# 50 Premium Christmas Holiday Cooking Recipes

By: Kelly Johnson

# Table of Contents

- Roasted Prime Rib with Garlic and Herb Crust
- Baked Ham with Brown Sugar and Mustard Glaze
- Stuffed Roast Turkey with Cranberry Orange Sauce
- Herb-Crusted Rack of Lamb
- Christmas Beef Wellington
- Honey Glazed Carrots
- Creamy Garlic Mashed Potatoes
- Brussels Sprouts with Bacon and Balsamic
- Chestnut and Sausage Stuffing
- Roasted Butternut Squash Soup
- Glazed Baby Carrots with Orange Zest
- Spinach and Ricotta Stuffed Mushrooms
- Sweet Potato Casserole with Marshmallows
- Gravy from Turkey Drippings
- Cranberry Sauce with Fresh Orange
- Baked Brie with Cranberry Chutney
- Cauliflower Gratin with Parmesan
- Herb-Infused Roasted Potatoes
- Roasted Brussels Sprouts with Balsamic Glaze
- Garlic Parmesan Green Beans
- Sauteed Mushrooms with Fresh Thyme
- Roasted Beet and Goat Cheese Salad
- Christmas Roast Duck with Cherry Sauce
- Twice-Baked Potatoes
- Pecan-Crusted Salmon
- Creamed Spinach
- Maple-Glazed Carrots
- Winter Vegetable Medley
- Parmesan Crusted Asparagus
- Wild Rice Pilaf with Cranberries
- Roasted Garlic and Herb Chicken
- Spinach and Artichoke Dip
- Shrimp Scampi
- Christmas Pudding
- Pumpkin Soup with Ginger Cream

- Sausage and Sage Stuffing
- Lobster Tail with Lemon Butter
- Grilled Pork Chops with Apple Chutney
- Christmas Eve Seafood Chowder
- Roasted Apple and Pear Salad
- Garlic Butter Lobster Tails
- Broccoli Rabe with Sausage
- Maple Bacon Brussels Sprouts
- Chocolate Peppermint Tart
- Gingerbread Pancakes
- Cinnamon Roll Casserole
- Hot Mulled Wine
- Classic Eggnog
- Focaccia Bread with Rosemary
- Christmas Sugar Cookies

# Roasted Prime Rib with Garlic and Herb Crust

**Ingredients:**

- 1 (4-5 lb) prime rib roast, bone-in
- 4 cloves garlic, minced
- 1/4 cup fresh rosemary, chopped
- 1/4 cup fresh thyme, chopped
- 1/4 cup olive oil
- 2 teaspoons kosher salt
- 1 teaspoon freshly ground black pepper
- 1 teaspoon Dijon mustard

**Instructions:**

1. **Prepare the roast**: Preheat your oven to 450°F (232°C). Place the prime rib roast on a roasting rack in a roasting pan.
2. **Make the herb crust**: In a bowl, combine garlic, rosemary, thyme, olive oil, salt, pepper, and Dijon mustard. Mix well.
3. **Coat the roast**: Rub the garlic and herb mixture all over the prime rib.
4. **Roast the meat**: Roast for 15 minutes at 450°F (232°C), then reduce the heat to 325°F (163°C). Continue roasting for about 1.5-2 hours or until the internal temperature reaches 125°F (for medium-rare).
5. **Rest and carve**: Let the roast rest for 15-20 minutes before carving. Serve with juices from the pan.

## Baked Ham with Brown Sugar and Mustard Glaze

**Ingredients:**

- 1 (6-8 lb) bone-in ham
- 1/2 cup brown sugar, packed
- 1/4 cup Dijon mustard
- 1/4 cup apple cider vinegar
- 1/4 cup maple syrup
- 1/4 teaspoon ground cloves

**Instructions:**

1. **Preheat the oven**: Heat oven to 325°F (163°C).
2. **Prepare the ham**: Score the surface of the ham in a diamond pattern and place it in a roasting pan.
3. **Make the glaze**: In a saucepan, combine brown sugar, mustard, vinegar, maple syrup, and ground cloves. Simmer for 5-7 minutes, stirring occasionally.
4. **Glaze the ham**: Brush the glaze over the ham, making sure to coat the entire surface.
5. **Roast the ham**: Bake for about 2 hours, basting the ham with more glaze every 30 minutes, until the ham reaches an internal temperature of 140°F (60°C).
6. **Serve**: Let rest for 10 minutes before slicing.

# Stuffed Roast Turkey with Cranberry Orange Sauce

**Ingredients for Turkey:**

- 1 (12-14 lb) whole turkey, thawed
- 1/4 cup olive oil or melted butter
- 1 tablespoon fresh rosemary, chopped
- 1 tablespoon fresh thyme, chopped
- Salt and pepper to taste
- 1/2 cup chicken broth

**Ingredients for Stuffing:**

- 1 loaf of bread, cubed
- 1/2 cup butter
- 1 onion, chopped
- 2 celery stalks, chopped
- 1/2 cup dried cranberries
- 1/2 cup chopped pecans
- 2 teaspoons fresh sage, chopped
- 1 1/2 cups chicken broth
- Salt and pepper to taste

**Ingredients for Cranberry Orange Sauce:**

- 1 bag (12 oz) fresh cranberries
- 1 cup sugar
- 1 cup orange juice
- Zest of one orange

**Instructions for Stuffing:**

1. **Make the stuffing**: In a large skillet, melt butter and sauté the onion and celery until soft. Add the bread cubes, cranberries, pecans, sage, chicken broth, salt, and pepper. Mix until everything is well combined. Set aside to cool.

**Instructions for Turkey:**

2. **Preheat the oven**: Heat oven to 325°F (163°C).
3. **Stuff the turkey**: Stuff the turkey with the prepared stuffing. Tie the legs together with kitchen twine and tuck the wings under the body.

4. **Season the turkey**: Rub the turkey with olive oil or melted butter, and sprinkle with rosemary, thyme, salt, and pepper.
5. **Roast the turkey**: Place the turkey on a roasting rack in a pan. Pour chicken broth into the pan and cover loosely with aluminum foil. Roast for 2.5-3 hours or until the internal temperature reaches 165°F (74°C).
6. **Make the sauce**: While the turkey is roasting, combine cranberries, sugar, orange juice, and zest in a saucepan. Simmer for 15 minutes until the cranberries burst and the sauce thickens.
7. **Serve**: Let the turkey rest before carving. Serve with cranberry orange sauce.

## Herb-Crusted Rack of Lamb

**Ingredients:**

- 1 (1.5-2 lb) rack of lamb, frenched
- 2 tablespoons olive oil
- 1/4 cup fresh rosemary, chopped
- 1/4 cup fresh thyme, chopped
- 3 cloves garlic, minced
- 1 teaspoon Dijon mustard
- Salt and pepper to taste

**Instructions:**

1. **Preheat the oven**: Heat oven to 400°F (204°C).
2. **Prepare the lamb**: Rub the rack of lamb with olive oil. In a small bowl, combine rosemary, thyme, garlic, mustard, salt, and pepper.
3. **Crust the lamb**: Rub the herb mixture all over the lamb.
4. **Roast the lamb**: Place the lamb on a roasting rack and roast for about 20-25 minutes, or until the internal temperature reaches 125°F (52°C) for medium-rare.
5. **Rest and serve**: Let rest for 10 minutes before slicing into individual chops.

## Christmas Beef Wellington

**Ingredients:**

- 1 (2 lb) beef tenderloin
- Salt and pepper to taste
- 2 tablespoons olive oil
- 8 oz mushrooms, finely chopped
- 2 tablespoons Dijon mustard
- 1/2 cup pâté (optional)
- 1 sheet puff pastry
- 1 egg, beaten

**Instructions:**

1. **Prepare the beef**: Preheat oven to 400°F (204°C). Season the beef tenderloin with salt and pepper.
2. **Sear the beef**: Heat olive oil in a skillet over high heat. Sear the beef on all sides until browned (about 2-3 minutes per side). Let cool.
3. **Prepare the mushroom duxelles**: Sauté the chopped mushrooms in the skillet until all moisture evaporates.
4. **Assemble the Wellington**: Spread Dijon mustard (and pâté, if using) on the beef, then top with the mushroom mixture. Wrap the beef in puff pastry, sealing the edges.
5. **Bake**: Brush with beaten egg and bake for 25-30 minutes, or until the pastry is golden and the internal temperature of the beef reaches 130°F (54°C) for medium-rare.
6. **Serve**: Let rest for 10 minutes before slicing.

## Honey Glazed Carrots

**Ingredients:**

- 1 lb baby carrots
- 2 tablespoons butter
- 2 tablespoons honey
- Salt and pepper to taste

**Instructions:**

1. **Cook the carrots**: Boil the carrots in salted water for about 8-10 minutes, or until tender.
2. **Make the glaze**: In a pan, melt butter and honey together.
3. **Glaze the carrots**: Drain the carrots and toss them in the honey glaze.
4. **Serve**: Season with salt and pepper and serve.

# Creamy Garlic Mashed Potatoes

**Ingredients:**

- 2 lb russet potatoes, peeled and cut into chunks
- 4 cloves garlic, minced
- 1/2 cup heavy cream
- 1/4 cup butter
- Salt and pepper to taste

**Instructions:**

1. **Cook the potatoes**: Boil the potatoes in salted water for 12-15 minutes, or until fork-tender.
2. **Mash the potatoes**: Drain and mash the potatoes.
3. **Make the garlic cream**: In a small saucepan, heat the cream, butter, and garlic until warm.
4. **Combine**: Stir the garlic cream into the mashed potatoes. Season with salt and pepper.
5. **Serve**: Serve immediately.

## Brussels Sprouts with Bacon and Balsamic

**Ingredients:**

- 1 lb Brussels sprouts, trimmed and halved
- 4 slices bacon, chopped
- 2 tablespoons balsamic vinegar
- Salt and pepper to taste

**Instructions:**

1. **Cook the bacon:** In a pan, cook bacon until crispy. Remove and set aside.
2. **Cook the Brussels sprouts:** In the same pan, sauté Brussels sprouts until golden and tender (about 8-10 minutes).
3. **Add vinegar and bacon:** Stir in balsamic vinegar and cooked bacon.
4. **Serve:** Season with salt and pepper before serving.

# Chestnut and Sausage Stuffing

**Ingredients:**

- 2 cups chestnuts, peeled and chopped
- 1 lb sausage (pork or turkey), crumbled
- 1 onion, chopped
- 2 celery stalks, chopped
- 4 cups cubed bread
- 1/2 cup chicken broth
- 1 teaspoon fresh sage, chopped
- Salt and pepper to taste

**Instructions:**

1. **Cook the sausage**: In a skillet, cook the sausage over medium heat until browned. Remove and set aside.
2. **Sauté the vegetables**: In the same skillet, cook the onion and celery until softened.
3. **Combine**: In a large bowl, combine chestnuts, sausage, sautéed vegetables, bread, and sage. Add chicken broth and mix well.
4. **Bake**: Transfer to a baking dish and bake at 350°F (175°C) for 25-30 minutes, until golden.
5. **Serve**: Season with salt and pepper and serve.

## Roasted Butternut Squash Soup

**Ingredients:**

- 1 medium butternut squash, peeled and cubed
- 1 tablespoon olive oil
- 1 onion, chopped
- 2 cloves garlic, minced
- 4 cups vegetable broth
- 1 teaspoon ground cinnamon
- 1/4 teaspoon ground nutmeg
- Salt and pepper to taste
- 1/2 cup heavy cream (optional)

**Instructions:**

1. **Roast the squash**: Preheat the oven to 400°F (200°C). Toss butternut squash cubes with olive oil, salt, and pepper. Roast on a baking sheet for 25-30 minutes, or until tender.
2. **Cook the aromatics**: In a large pot, sauté onion and garlic until soft, about 5 minutes.
3. **Blend the soup**: Add the roasted squash to the pot along with cinnamon, nutmeg, and vegetable broth. Bring to a boil, then reduce heat and simmer for 10 minutes.
4. **Puree**: Use an immersion blender to puree the soup until smooth. Alternatively, blend in batches in a countertop blender.
5. **Finish the soup**: Stir in the heavy cream (if using), and adjust seasoning with salt and pepper.
6. **Serve**: Ladle into bowls and garnish with a drizzle of cream or a sprinkle of cinnamon.

## Glazed Baby Carrots with Orange Zest

**Ingredients:**

- 1 lb baby carrots, peeled
- 2 tablespoons butter
- 2 tablespoons honey
- Zest of 1 orange
- Salt and pepper to taste

**Instructions:**

1. **Cook the carrots**: Bring a pot of salted water to a boil and cook the baby carrots for about 8-10 minutes, or until tender. Drain.
2. **Glaze the carrots**: In a skillet, melt butter over medium heat. Add honey and stir in orange zest. Let the glaze simmer for 2-3 minutes.
3. **Toss and serve**: Add the cooked carrots to the skillet and toss to coat with the glaze. Season with salt and pepper, then serve.

# Spinach and Ricotta Stuffed Mushrooms

**Ingredients:**

- 16 large mushroom caps, stems removed
- 1 cup fresh spinach, chopped
- 1/2 cup ricotta cheese
- 1/4 cup grated Parmesan cheese
- 1/4 cup breadcrumbs
- 2 cloves garlic, minced
- 1 tablespoon olive oil
- Salt and pepper to taste

**Instructions:**

1. **Preheat the oven**: Heat oven to 375°F (190°C).
2. **Prepare the filling**: In a skillet, sauté garlic in olive oil for 1-2 minutes until fragrant. Add spinach and cook until wilted.
3. **Mix the stuffing**: In a bowl, combine the spinach mixture, ricotta, Parmesan, breadcrumbs, salt, and pepper.
4. **Stuff the mushrooms**: Spoon the filling into the mushroom caps and place them on a baking sheet.
5. **Bake**: Bake for 20-25 minutes, or until the mushrooms are tender and the filling is golden.
6. **Serve**: Serve immediately as an appetizer or side dish.

## Sweet Potato Casserole with Marshmallows

**Ingredients:**

- 4 medium sweet potatoes, peeled and cubed
- 1/2 cup brown sugar
- 1/4 cup butter, melted
- 1/2 cup milk
- 1 teaspoon vanilla extract
- 1/4 teaspoon ground cinnamon
- 1/4 teaspoon ground nutmeg
- 1 1/2 cups mini marshmallows

**Instructions:**

1. **Cook the sweet potatoes**: Boil the cubed sweet potatoes in a large pot of salted water until tender, about 10-12 minutes. Drain and mash.
2. **Make the casserole**: In a bowl, combine the mashed sweet potatoes with brown sugar, butter, milk, vanilla, cinnamon, and nutmeg. Mix until smooth.
3. **Top with marshmallows**: Transfer the mixture into a greased casserole dish and top with mini marshmallows.
4. **Bake**: Preheat oven to 350°F (175°C) and bake for 20 minutes, or until the marshmallows are golden brown.
5. **Serve**: Serve as a side dish for Thanksgiving or a holiday meal.

## Gravy from Turkey Drippings

**Ingredients:**

- 1/4 cup turkey drippings
- 1/4 cup all-purpose flour
- 2 cups turkey or chicken broth
- Salt and pepper to taste

**Instructions:**

1. **Make the roux**: In a saucepan, heat turkey drippings over medium heat. Whisk in the flour and cook for 2-3 minutes, until it forms a paste.
2. **Add the broth**: Gradually whisk in the broth, stirring constantly to prevent lumps.
3. **Simmer the gravy**: Bring the mixture to a boil, then reduce heat and simmer for 5-7 minutes, or until thickened.
4. **Season and serve**: Season with salt and pepper to taste, then serve over turkey.

# Cranberry Sauce with Fresh Orange

**Ingredients:**

- 1 bag (12 oz) fresh cranberries
- 1 cup sugar
- 1 cup orange juice
- Zest of 1 orange

**Instructions:**

1. **Cook the cranberries**: In a saucepan, combine cranberries, sugar, and orange juice. Bring to a boil, then reduce to a simmer.
2. **Simmer**: Cook for 10-15 minutes, or until the cranberries burst and the sauce thickens.
3. **Add zest**: Stir in the orange zest.
4. **Cool and serve**: Let the sauce cool to room temperature before serving.

## Baked Brie with Cranberry Chutney

**Ingredients:**

- 1 wheel of Brie cheese (8 oz)
- 1/2 cup cranberry chutney
- 1 tablespoon chopped pecans (optional)
- 1 tablespoon honey (optional)
- Crackers or baguette slices for serving

**Instructions:**

1. **Preheat the oven**: Heat oven to 350°F (175°C).
2. **Prepare the Brie**: Place the Brie wheel on a baking dish and bake for 10-12 minutes, or until soft and warm.
3. **Top with chutney**: Remove from oven and top with cranberry chutney, honey, and pecans.
4. **Serve**: Serve with crackers or slices of baguette.

## Cauliflower Gratin with Parmesan

**Ingredients:**

- 1 head of cauliflower, cut into florets
- 2 tablespoons butter
- 1/4 cup all-purpose flour
- 2 cups milk
- 1 cup shredded Parmesan cheese
- 1/2 teaspoon garlic powder
- Salt and pepper to taste
- 1/2 cup breadcrumbs

**Instructions:**

1. **Cook the cauliflower**: Boil or steam the cauliflower florets until tender, about 6-8 minutes. Drain well.
2. **Make the sauce**: In a saucepan, melt butter over medium heat. Whisk in flour and cook for 2-3 minutes. Gradually add milk, whisking constantly. Cook until thickened.
3. **Add cheese and seasonings**: Stir in Parmesan, garlic powder, salt, and pepper.
4. **Assemble the gratin**: Place the cauliflower in a greased baking dish and pour the sauce over it. Sprinkle breadcrumbs on top.
5. **Bake**: Preheat oven to 350°F (175°C) and bake for 20 minutes, or until golden and bubbly.
6. **Serve**: Serve hot as a side dish.

**Herb-Infused Roasted Potatoes**

**Ingredients:**

- 2 lbs baby potatoes, halved
- 2 tablespoons olive oil
- 1 teaspoon fresh rosemary, chopped
- 1 teaspoon fresh thyme, chopped
- 2 cloves garlic, minced
- Salt and pepper to taste

**Instructions:**

1. **Preheat the oven**: Heat oven to 400°F (200°C).
2. **Prepare the potatoes**: Toss the potatoes with olive oil, rosemary, thyme, garlic, salt, and pepper.
3. **Roast**: Spread the potatoes in a single layer on a baking sheet. Roast for 25-30 minutes, or until golden and tender.
4. **Serve**: Serve hot as a side dish.

## Roasted Brussels Sprouts with Balsamic Glaze

### Ingredients:

- 1 lb Brussels sprouts, trimmed and halved
- 2 tablespoons olive oil
- Salt and pepper to taste
- 1/4 cup balsamic vinegar
- 1 tablespoon honey

### Instructions:

1. **Preheat the oven**: Heat oven to 400°F (200°C).
2. **Roast the Brussels sprouts**: Toss Brussels sprouts with olive oil, salt, and pepper. Roast on a baking sheet for 20-25 minutes, or until golden brown and crispy.
3. **Make the glaze**: In a small saucepan, simmer balsamic vinegar and honey until thickened, about 5 minutes.
4. **Serve**: Drizzle the balsamic glaze over the roasted Brussels sprouts and serve.

# Garlic Parmesan Green Beans

**Ingredients:**

- 1 lb fresh green beans, trimmed
- 2 tablespoons olive oil
- 3 cloves garlic, minced
- 1/4 cup grated Parmesan cheese
- Salt and pepper to taste
- 1 tablespoon lemon juice (optional)

**Instructions:**

1. **Blanch the green beans**: Bring a pot of salted water to a boil. Add the green beans and cook for 4-5 minutes until tender-crisp. Drain and set aside.
2. **Sauté the garlic**: Heat olive oil in a large skillet over medium heat. Add the garlic and sauté for 1-2 minutes until fragrant.
3. **Toss the beans**: Add the blanched green beans to the skillet and toss to coat in the garlic oil.
4. **Finish**: Sprinkle with Parmesan cheese, salt, pepper, and a squeeze of lemon juice if desired. Toss to combine and serve immediately.

**Sauteed Mushrooms with Fresh Thyme**

**Ingredients:**

- 1 lb mushrooms, sliced
- 2 tablespoons butter
- 1 tablespoon olive oil
- 2 cloves garlic, minced
- 1 tablespoon fresh thyme, chopped
- Salt and pepper to taste

**Instructions:**

1. **Cook the mushrooms**: Heat butter and olive oil in a skillet over medium-high heat. Add the mushrooms and cook for 8-10 minutes, stirring occasionally, until the mushrooms release their moisture and become golden brown.
2. **Add garlic and thyme**: Add garlic and fresh thyme to the skillet, and cook for 1-2 minutes until fragrant.
3. **Season and serve**: Season with salt and pepper, then serve immediately as a side dish.

## Roasted Beet and Goat Cheese Salad

**Ingredients:**

- 4 medium beets, peeled and cubed
- 2 tablespoons olive oil
- Salt and pepper to taste
- 2 cups mixed greens (arugula, spinach, etc.)
- 4 oz goat cheese, crumbled
- 1/4 cup walnuts, toasted (optional)
- Balsamic vinaigrette (to taste)

**Instructions:**

1. **Roast the beets**: Preheat the oven to 400°F (200°C). Toss the beet cubes with olive oil, salt, and pepper. Roast on a baking sheet for 30-35 minutes, or until tender.
2. **Assemble the salad**: In a large bowl, combine mixed greens, roasted beets, crumbled goat cheese, and toasted walnuts (if using).
3. **Dress the salad**: Drizzle with balsamic vinaigrette and toss gently to combine. Serve immediately.

# Christmas Roast Duck with Cherry Sauce

**Ingredients:**

- 1 whole duck (about 5 lbs)
- Salt and pepper to taste
- 1 tablespoon olive oil
- 1/2 cup red wine
- 1 cup chicken broth
- 2 tablespoons balsamic vinegar
- 1/2 cup fresh cherries, pitted
- 1 tablespoon honey

**Instructions:**

1. **Preheat the oven**: Preheat oven to 375°F (190°C).
2. **Season the duck**: Pat the duck dry with paper towels and season generously with salt and pepper.
3. **Roast the duck**: Place the duck in a roasting pan, breast side up. Roast for about 2 hours, or until the skin is golden and crispy.
4. **Make the cherry sauce**: While the duck is roasting, combine red wine, chicken broth, balsamic vinegar, cherries, and honey in a saucepan. Bring to a boil, then simmer for 10-15 minutes until thickened.
5. **Serve**: Once the duck is done, let it rest for 10 minutes before carving. Serve with the cherry sauce.

## Twice-Baked Potatoes

**Ingredients:**

- 4 large russet potatoes
- 1/2 cup sour cream
- 1/2 cup shredded cheddar cheese
- 1/4 cup milk
- 2 tablespoons butter
- 2 green onions, chopped
- Salt and pepper to taste

**Instructions:**

1. **Bake the potatoes**: Preheat oven to 400°F (200°C). Pierce the potatoes with a fork and bake directly on the oven rack for 45-50 minutes, or until tender.
2. **Scoop out the potatoes**: Let the potatoes cool slightly, then cut them in half and scoop out the flesh, leaving a thin border.
3. **Mash the filling**: Mash the potato flesh with sour cream, cheese, milk, butter, green onions, salt, and pepper until smooth.
4. **Refill the skins**: Spoon the mashed potato mixture back into the potato skins.
5. **Bake again**: Place the stuffed potatoes back in the oven and bake for 15-20 minutes, or until golden on top.
6. **Serve**: Serve as a hearty side dish.

## Pecan-Crusted Salmon

**Ingredients:**

- 4 salmon fillets
- 1/2 cup crushed pecans
- 1/4 cup breadcrumbs
- 1 tablespoon Dijon mustard
- 1 tablespoon olive oil
- Salt and pepper to taste

**Instructions:**

1. **Preheat the oven**: Preheat oven to 375°F (190°C).
2. **Prepare the crust**: In a bowl, combine crushed pecans, breadcrumbs, salt, and pepper.
3. **Coat the salmon**: Brush each salmon fillet with Dijon mustard, then press it into the pecan mixture to coat.
4. **Bake**: Place the salmon fillets on a baking sheet and drizzle with olive oil. Bake for 15-20 minutes, or until the salmon is cooked through and the crust is golden.
5. **Serve**: Serve hot with your favorite sides.

## Creamed Spinach

**Ingredients:**

- 1 lb fresh spinach, chopped
- 2 tablespoons butter
- 1/4 cup onion, chopped
- 2 cloves garlic, minced
- 1/2 cup heavy cream
- 1/4 cup grated Parmesan cheese
- Salt and pepper to taste

**Instructions:**

1. **Cook the spinach**: In a large skillet, cook the spinach in batches until wilted, then drain excess liquid.
2. **Sauté the onions and garlic**: In the same skillet, melt butter and sauté onions and garlic for 3-4 minutes.
3. **Make the cream sauce**: Add heavy cream and bring to a simmer. Stir in Parmesan cheese and cook for 3-4 minutes, until thickened.
4. **Combine and serve**: Add the spinach back into the skillet, stir to combine, and season with salt and pepper. Serve warm.

## Maple-Glazed Carrots

**Ingredients:**

- 1 lb baby carrots, peeled
- 2 tablespoons butter
- 2 tablespoons maple syrup
- Salt and pepper to taste
- Fresh parsley, chopped (optional)

**Instructions:**

1. **Cook the carrots**: Boil or steam the baby carrots until tender, about 8-10 minutes. Drain.
2. **Glaze the carrots**: In a skillet, melt butter over medium heat. Add maple syrup and stir. Let simmer for 2-3 minutes.
3. **Toss the carrots**: Add the carrots to the skillet and toss to coat with the glaze.
4. **Serve**: Season with salt and pepper, and sprinkle with parsley, if desired. Serve immediately.

## Winter Vegetable Medley

**Ingredients:**

- 1 cup carrots, sliced
- 1 cup parsnips, sliced
- 1 cup Brussels sprouts, halved
- 1 tablespoon olive oil
- 1 teaspoon fresh thyme
- Salt and pepper to taste

**Instructions:**

1. **Preheat the oven**: Heat oven to 400°F (200°C).
2. **Prepare the vegetables**: Toss carrots, parsnips, and Brussels sprouts with olive oil, thyme, salt, and pepper.
3. **Roast**: Spread vegetables on a baking sheet in a single layer. Roast for 25-30 minutes, stirring halfway through, until tender and golden.
4. **Serve**: Serve as a warm side dish for any holiday meal.

**Parmesan Crusted Asparagus**

**Ingredients:**

- 1 lb fresh asparagus, trimmed
- 1/4 cup grated Parmesan cheese
- 1/4 cup breadcrumbs
- 1 tablespoon olive oil
- Salt and pepper to taste

**Instructions:**

1. **Preheat the oven**: Heat oven to 400°F (200°C).
2. **Prepare the asparagus**: Arrange asparagus on a baking sheet. Drizzle with olive oil and season with salt and pepper.
3. **Top with Parmesan**: Sprinkle Parmesan cheese and breadcrumbs over the asparagus.
4. **Bake**: Roast for 12-15 minutes, or until the asparagus is tender and the crust is golden.
5. **Serve**: Serve immediately as a side dish.

**Wild Rice Pilaf with Cranberries**

**Ingredients:**

- 1 cup wild rice
- 2 cups chicken or vegetable broth
- 1/2 cup dried cranberries
- 1/4 cup chopped onion
- 1/4 cup chopped celery
- 1/4 cup chopped carrots
- 2 tablespoons olive oil
- 1 tablespoon fresh parsley, chopped
- Salt and pepper to taste

**Instructions:**

1. **Cook the rice**: In a large pot, bring the broth to a boil. Add the wild rice, reduce the heat, and simmer for 35-40 minutes, until the rice is tender and the liquid is absorbed.
2. **Sauté the vegetables**: In a skillet, heat olive oil over medium heat. Add the onion, celery, and carrots, and cook for 5-7 minutes until softened.
3. **Combine**: Add the sautéed vegetables and dried cranberries to the cooked rice, and stir to combine. Season with salt and pepper.
4. **Finish**: Sprinkle with fresh parsley and serve warm.

## Roasted Garlic and Herb Chicken

**Ingredients:**

- 1 whole chicken (about 4 lbs)
- 2 tablespoons olive oil
- 4 cloves garlic, minced
- 1 tablespoon fresh rosemary, chopped
- 1 tablespoon fresh thyme, chopped
- 1 tablespoon lemon zest
- Salt and pepper to taste

**Instructions:**

1. **Preheat the oven**: Preheat the oven to 375°F (190°C).
2. **Prepare the chicken**: Pat the chicken dry with paper towels. Rub olive oil all over the skin, then sprinkle with garlic, rosemary, thyme, lemon zest, salt, and pepper.
3. **Roast the chicken**: Place the chicken on a roasting pan, breast side up. Roast for about 1 hour and 15 minutes, or until the internal temperature reaches 165°F (75°C).
4. **Rest and serve**: Let the chicken rest for 10 minutes before carving. Serve with roasted vegetables or a side dish of your choice.

## Spinach and Artichoke Dip

**Ingredients:**

- 1 cup frozen spinach, thawed and drained
- 1 can (14 oz) artichoke hearts, drained and chopped
- 1/2 cup sour cream
- 1/2 cup mayonnaise
- 1/2 cup grated Parmesan cheese
- 1/2 cup shredded mozzarella cheese
- 1/4 teaspoon garlic powder
- Salt and pepper to taste

**Instructions:**

1. **Preheat the oven**: Preheat the oven to 375°F (190°C).
2. **Mix the dip**: In a bowl, combine spinach, artichokes, sour cream, mayonnaise, Parmesan cheese, mozzarella cheese, garlic powder, salt, and pepper.
3. **Bake the dip**: Transfer the mixture to a baking dish and bake for 25-30 minutes, or until bubbly and golden on top.
4. **Serve**: Serve warm with crackers, bread, or vegetable sticks for dipping.

## Shrimp Scampi

**Ingredients:**

- 1 lb large shrimp, peeled and deveined
- 4 cloves garlic, minced
- 2 tablespoons butter
- 2 tablespoons olive oil
- 1/2 cup dry white wine
- 1 tablespoon lemon juice
- 1/4 cup chopped fresh parsley
- Salt and pepper to taste
- 8 oz pasta (linguine or spaghetti)

**Instructions:**

1. **Cook the pasta**: Cook the pasta according to package instructions, drain, and set aside.
2. **Sauté the shrimp**: In a large skillet, melt butter and olive oil over medium heat. Add the garlic and cook for 1 minute. Add the shrimp and cook for 3-4 minutes until pink and opaque.
3. **Make the sauce**: Add the white wine and lemon juice to the skillet, scraping the bottom to deglaze the pan. Cook for 2-3 minutes, reducing the sauce slightly.
4. **Combine and serve**: Add the cooked pasta to the skillet, tossing to coat in the sauce. Stir in parsley and season with salt and pepper. Serve immediately.

# Christmas Pudding

**Ingredients:**

- 1 cup dried currants
- 1 cup raisins
- 1/2 cup chopped dried apricots
- 1/2 cup chopped candied ginger
- 1/4 cup brandy or rum
- 1 cup breadcrumbs
- 1/2 cup suet (or vegetable shortening)
- 1/2 cup brown sugar
- 2 large eggs
- 1/2 teaspoon ground cinnamon
- 1/2 teaspoon ground nutmeg
- 1/4 teaspoon ground allspice
- 1/4 cup milk

**Instructions:**

1. **Soak the fruits**: In a bowl, soak currants, raisins, apricots, and ginger in brandy or rum for at least 1 hour.
2. **Mix the batter**: In a separate bowl, combine breadcrumbs, suet, brown sugar, eggs, spices, and milk. Stir in the soaked fruits and any remaining soaking liquid.
3. **Steam the pudding**: Grease a pudding basin or heatproof bowl. Pour the mixture into the basin and cover with parchment paper. Steam over simmering water for about 2 hours, checking the water level occasionally.
4. **Serve**: Let the pudding cool slightly before serving with custard or whipped cream.

## Pumpkin Soup with Ginger Cream

### Ingredients:

- 4 cups pumpkin puree (fresh or canned)
- 4 cups vegetable broth
- 1 onion, chopped
- 2 cloves garlic, minced
- 1 teaspoon ground ginger
- 1/2 teaspoon cinnamon
- 1/2 teaspoon nutmeg
- 1/2 cup heavy cream
- Salt and pepper to taste
- 1 tablespoon olive oil

### Instructions:

1. **Sauté the aromatics**: In a large pot, heat olive oil over medium heat. Add the onion and garlic and sauté for 5-7 minutes until softened.
2. **Simmer the soup**: Add the pumpkin puree, vegetable broth, ginger, cinnamon, and nutmeg. Stir to combine, and bring to a simmer. Cook for 15-20 minutes to let the flavors meld.
3. **Blend**: Use an immersion blender to puree the soup until smooth. Season with salt and pepper to taste.
4. **Make the ginger cream**: Whisk the heavy cream with a pinch of ground ginger.
5. **Serve**: Ladle the soup into bowls and drizzle with the ginger cream.

## Sausage and Sage Stuffing

**Ingredients:**

- 1 lb Italian sausage, casing removed
- 1 onion, chopped
- 2 celery stalks, chopped
- 1/2 cup chicken broth
- 1 tablespoon fresh sage, chopped
- 1 teaspoon dried thyme
- 6 cups cubed bread (preferably day-old)
- Salt and pepper to taste

**Instructions:**

1. **Cook the sausage**: In a large skillet, brown the sausage over medium heat, breaking it into pieces. Remove from the skillet and set aside.
2. **Sauté the vegetables**: In the same skillet, sauté the onion and celery until softened, about 5 minutes.
3. **Combine the stuffing**: In a large bowl, combine the bread cubes, cooked sausage, sautéed vegetables, sage, thyme, and chicken broth. Mix well and season with salt and pepper.
4. **Bake**: Transfer the stuffing mixture to a greased baking dish and bake at 350°F (175°C) for 25-30 minutes, or until golden and crispy on top.

## Lobster Tail with Lemon Butter

**Ingredients:**

- 4 lobster tails
- 4 tablespoons butter, melted
- 2 tablespoons lemon juice
- 1 tablespoon garlic, minced
- Salt and pepper to taste
- Fresh parsley, chopped (for garnish)

**Instructions:**

1. **Prepare the lobster tails**: Using kitchen scissors, cut through the top shell of each lobster tail, then gently pull the meat out and place it on top of the shell.
2. **Make the lemon butter**: In a small bowl, combine melted butter, lemon juice, garlic, salt, and pepper.
3. **Bake the lobster**: Preheat the oven to 375°F (190°C). Place the lobster tails on a baking sheet and brush them with the lemon butter mixture.
4. **Bake**: Bake for 12-15 minutes, or until the lobster meat is opaque and tender.
5. **Serve**: Garnish with fresh parsley and serve immediately.

# Grilled Pork Chops with Apple Chutney

**Ingredients:**

- 4 bone-in pork chops
- Salt and pepper to taste
- 2 tablespoons olive oil
- 1 tablespoon fresh rosemary, chopped
- 2 apples, peeled, cored, and chopped
- 1/4 cup apple cider vinegar
- 1 tablespoon brown sugar
- 1/4 teaspoon cinnamon
- 1/4 teaspoon ground cloves

**Instructions:**

1. **Grill the pork chops**: Season the pork chops with salt, pepper, and rosemary. Preheat the grill to medium-high heat. Grill the pork chops for 6-8 minutes per side until cooked through.
2. **Make the chutney**: In a small saucepan, combine apples, apple cider vinegar, brown sugar, cinnamon, and cloves. Bring to a simmer over medium heat and cook for 10-12 minutes until the apples are soft and the sauce thickens.
3. **Serve**: Spoon the apple chutney over the grilled pork chops and serve immediately.

# Christmas Eve Seafood Chowder

**Ingredients:**

- 1 lb shrimp, peeled and deveined
- 1 lb scallops
- 1 lb white fish fillets (such as cod or haddock), cut into chunks
- 4 cups seafood stock
- 2 cups heavy cream
- 1 medium onion, chopped
- 2 celery stalks, chopped
- 2 carrots, peeled and diced
- 4 medium potatoes, peeled and diced
- 3 cloves garlic, minced
- 2 tablespoons butter
- 1 teaspoon fresh thyme, chopped
- 1/2 teaspoon ground white pepper
- Salt to taste
- Fresh parsley, chopped (for garnish)

**Instructions:**

1. **Sauté the vegetables**: In a large pot, melt butter over medium heat. Add onion, celery, carrots, and garlic. Sauté for 5-7 minutes until the vegetables begin to soften.
2. **Cook the potatoes**: Add the diced potatoes, seafood stock, thyme, and white pepper. Bring to a simmer and cook for about 10 minutes, or until the potatoes are tender.
3. **Add the seafood**: Add the shrimp, scallops, and fish to the pot. Cook for an additional 5-7 minutes, or until the seafood is cooked through.
4. **Add the cream**: Stir in the heavy cream and bring to a gentle simmer. Season with salt to taste.
5. **Serve**: Ladle the chowder into bowls, and garnish with fresh parsley.

## Roasted Apple and Pear Salad

**Ingredients:**

- 2 apples, cored and sliced
- 2 pears, cored and sliced
- 1 tablespoon olive oil
- 1 tablespoon honey
- 1 teaspoon cinnamon
- 4 cups mixed greens (such as arugula, spinach, or baby kale)
- 1/4 cup crumbled goat cheese
- 1/4 cup chopped walnuts, toasted
- 1/4 cup balsamic vinaigrette

**Instructions:**

1. **Roast the fruit**: Preheat the oven to 375°F (190°C). Toss the apple and pear slices with olive oil, honey, and cinnamon. Spread them on a baking sheet and roast for 15-20 minutes, or until tender and lightly caramelized.
2. **Assemble the salad**: In a large bowl, combine the mixed greens, roasted fruit, goat cheese, and toasted walnuts.
3. **Dress the salad**: Drizzle with balsamic vinaigrette and toss gently to combine.
4. **Serve**: Serve immediately as a fresh and vibrant holiday salad.

## Garlic Butter Lobster Tails

**Ingredients:**

- 4 lobster tails
- 1/2 cup butter, melted
- 4 cloves garlic, minced
- 1 tablespoon fresh lemon juice
- 1 tablespoon chopped fresh parsley
- Salt and pepper to taste

**Instructions:**

1. **Prepare the lobster tails**: Use kitchen scissors to cut the top of the lobster shells lengthwise. Carefully pull the lobster meat out and place it on top of the shell.
2. **Make the garlic butter**: In a small bowl, combine melted butter, minced garlic, lemon juice, parsley, salt, and pepper.
3. **Broil the lobster**: Preheat the broiler. Place the lobster tails on a baking sheet and brush generously with the garlic butter. Broil for 8-10 minutes, or until the lobster meat is opaque and lightly browned on top.
4. **Serve**: Serve the lobster tails with extra garlic butter and lemon wedges on the side.

## Broccoli Rabe with Sausage

**Ingredients:**

- 1 bunch broccoli rabe, trimmed
- 1 lb Italian sausage (mild or spicy, based on preference)
- 4 cloves garlic, minced
- 1/4 teaspoon red pepper flakes (optional)
- 2 tablespoons olive oil
- Salt and pepper to taste

**Instructions:**

1. **Cook the sausage**: In a large skillet, heat 1 tablespoon of olive oil over medium heat. Add the sausage, breaking it into smaller pieces as it cooks. Cook for 8-10 minutes, or until browned and cooked through. Remove from the pan and set aside.
2. **Sauté the garlic and broccoli rabe**: In the same skillet, add the remaining tablespoon of olive oil. Add garlic and red pepper flakes (if using) and cook for 1-2 minutes until fragrant. Add the broccoli rabe and cook, stirring occasionally, for about 5 minutes, or until wilted and tender.
3. **Combine and serve**: Return the sausage to the skillet and stir everything together. Season with salt and pepper to taste, and serve immediately.

# Maple Bacon Brussels Sprouts

**Ingredients:**

- 1 lb Brussels sprouts, trimmed and halved
- 6 slices bacon, chopped
- 2 tablespoons maple syrup
- 1 tablespoon balsamic vinegar
- Salt and pepper to taste

**Instructions:**

1. **Cook the bacon:** In a large skillet, cook the chopped bacon over medium heat until crispy, about 6-8 minutes. Remove the bacon and set it aside, leaving the rendered bacon fat in the skillet.
2. **Sauté the Brussels sprouts:** Add the halved Brussels sprouts to the skillet and cook, stirring occasionally, for 6-8 minutes, until they are golden brown and tender.
3. **Add the maple syrup:** Drizzle the maple syrup and balsamic vinegar over the Brussels sprouts, stirring to coat. Cook for another 2 minutes to let the flavors combine.
4. **Finish and serve:** Stir in the cooked bacon, season with salt and pepper, and serve warm.

## Chocolate Peppermint Tart

**Ingredients:**

- 1 pre-made chocolate tart crust (or homemade)
- 8 oz dark chocolate, chopped
- 1/2 cup heavy cream
- 1 teaspoon peppermint extract
- 1/4 cup crushed peppermint candies or candy canes
- Whipped cream, for serving (optional)

**Instructions:**

1. **Make the ganache**: In a small saucepan, heat the heavy cream over medium heat until just simmering. Pour the hot cream over the chopped dark chocolate and let sit for 2-3 minutes to melt. Stir until smooth, then add the peppermint extract and mix well.
2. **Fill the tart shell**: Pour the chocolate ganache into the pre-baked tart crust and smooth out the top with a spatula.
3. **Chill**: Place the tart in the refrigerator for at least 2 hours to allow the ganache to set.
4. **Garnish and serve**: Once set, sprinkle the top with crushed peppermint candies. Serve with a dollop of whipped cream if desired.

## Gingerbread Pancakes

**Ingredients:**

- 1 1/2 cups all-purpose flour
- 2 tablespoons brown sugar
- 1 tablespoon ground ginger
- 1 teaspoon ground cinnamon
- 1/2 teaspoon ground nutmeg
- 1/4 teaspoon ground cloves
- 1 teaspoon baking powder
- 1/2 teaspoon baking soda
- 1/4 teaspoon salt
- 1 cup buttermilk
- 1 large egg
- 2 tablespoons molasses
- 2 tablespoons melted butter
- 1 teaspoon vanilla extract

**Instructions:**

1. **Prepare the batter**: In a large bowl, whisk together the flour, brown sugar, spices, baking powder, baking soda, and salt.
2. **Mix the wet ingredients**: In a separate bowl, whisk together the buttermilk, egg, molasses, melted butter, and vanilla extract.
3. **Combine**: Pour the wet ingredients into the dry ingredients and stir until just combined (be careful not to overmix).
4. **Cook the pancakes**: Heat a nonstick skillet or griddle over medium heat and lightly grease with butter or cooking spray. Pour 1/4 cup of batter onto the skillet for each pancake. Cook for 2-3 minutes on each side, or until golden brown.
5. **Serve**: Serve warm with syrup, whipped cream, or fresh fruit.

## Cinnamon Roll Casserole

**Ingredients:**

- 2 cans refrigerated cinnamon rolls (with icing)
- 3 large eggs
- 1 cup heavy cream
- 1/2 cup milk
- 1 teaspoon vanilla extract
- 1/4 teaspoon ground cinnamon
- 1/4 teaspoon ground nutmeg
- 1/4 teaspoon salt
- 1/2 cup chopped pecans (optional)

**Instructions:**

1. **Prepare the casserole**: Preheat the oven to 350°F (175°C). Grease a 9x13-inch baking dish.
2. **Arrange the cinnamon rolls**: Cut each cinnamon roll into quarters and arrange them in the prepared baking dish.
3. **Make the custard**: In a large bowl, whisk together the eggs, heavy cream, milk, vanilla extract, cinnamon, nutmeg, and salt. Pour the custard mixture over the cinnamon rolls, making sure to coat them evenly.
4. **Top with pecans**: If using, sprinkle the chopped pecans on top.
5. **Bake**: Bake for 30-35 minutes, or until the casserole is golden brown and the center is set.
6. **Serve**: Drizzle with the icing from the cinnamon roll cans, or add your favorite glaze, and serve warm.

## Hot Mulled Wine

**Ingredients:**

- 1 bottle red wine (750 ml)
- 1/4 cup brandy
- 1/4 cup honey or sugar (to taste)
- 1 orange, sliced
- 1 lemon, sliced
- 3 cinnamon sticks
- 5 cloves
- 2 star anise (optional)

**Instructions:**

1. **Heat the wine**: In a large pot, combine the wine, brandy, honey (or sugar), orange slices, lemon slices, cinnamon sticks, cloves, and star anise (if using).
2. **Simmer**: Heat the mixture over low heat, stirring occasionally until hot (but not boiling). Let it simmer for 20-30 minutes to allow the flavors to meld.
3. **Serve**: Strain the mulled wine into mugs, discarding the solids. Serve warm.

## Classic Eggnog

**Ingredients:**

- 6 large egg yolks
- 3/4 cup granulated sugar
- 2 cups whole milk
- 1 1/2 cups heavy cream
- 1 teaspoon vanilla extract
- 1 teaspoon ground nutmeg
- 1/2 teaspoon ground cinnamon
- 1/2 cup dark rum (optional)
- 1/2 cup bourbon (optional)
- 6 large egg whites (optional, for a frothy texture)

**Instructions:**

1. **Make the custard**: In a large bowl, whisk the egg yolks and sugar together until thick and pale.
2. **Heat the milk and cream**: In a saucepan, combine the milk and cream. Heat over medium heat until it is steaming but not boiling.
3. **Combine and cook**: Gradually pour the hot milk mixture into the egg mixture, whisking constantly. Return the mixture to the pot and cook over low heat, stirring constantly, until it thickens slightly (about 5-7 minutes).
4. **Chill the eggnog**: Remove from heat and stir in the vanilla, nutmeg, and cinnamon. Let the mixture cool, then refrigerate for at least 2 hours.
5. **Optional froth**: If using, whisk the egg whites until soft peaks form and fold them into the eggnog just before serving for a frothy texture.
6. **Serve**: Pour into glasses and, if desired, stir in rum and bourbon. Garnish with extra nutmeg before serving.

## Focaccia Bread with Rosemary

**Ingredients:**

- 2 cups all-purpose flour
- 1 packet (2 1/4 teaspoons) active dry yeast
- 1 teaspoon salt
- 1 tablespoon sugar
- 3/4 cup warm water
- 2 tablespoons olive oil, plus more for drizzling
- 2 tablespoons fresh rosemary, chopped
- Coarse sea salt for sprinkling

**Instructions:**

1. **Activate the yeast**: In a bowl, combine the warm water, sugar, and yeast. Let sit for about 5 minutes, until it becomes frothy.
2. **Make the dough**: In a large bowl, mix the flour and salt. Add the yeast mixture and 2 tablespoons of olive oil. Stir until the dough comes together, then knead for about 5-7 minutes until smooth.
3. **First rise**: Place the dough in a lightly oiled bowl, cover with a damp cloth, and let it rise for 1 hour, or until doubled in size.
4. **Shape the dough**: Preheat the oven to 400°F (200°C). Punch down the dough and transfer it to a baking sheet. Press it out into a rectangle.
5. **Second rise and bake**: Cover with a cloth and let it rise for 20-30 minutes. Once risen, drizzle with olive oil, sprinkle with chopped rosemary, and sprinkle with sea salt.
6. **Bake**: Bake for 20-25 minutes, or until golden brown. Serve warm.

## Christmas Sugar Cookies

**Ingredients:**

- 2 3/4 cups all-purpose flour
- 1 teaspoon baking soda
- 1 teaspoon cream of tartar
- 1/2 teaspoon salt
- 1 cup unsalted butter, softened
- 1 1/2 cups granulated sugar, divided
- 1 large egg
- 1 teaspoon vanilla extract
- 1 teaspoon almond extract (optional)

**Instructions:**

1. **Prepare the dough**: Preheat the oven to 350°F (175°C). In a medium bowl, combine the flour, baking soda, cream of tartar, and salt. Set aside.
2. **Cream the butter and sugar**: In a large bowl, cream the softened butter with 1 cup of sugar until light and fluffy. Beat in the egg and vanilla (and almond extract, if using).
3. **Mix the dry ingredients**: Gradually add the dry ingredients to the butter mixture, mixing until combined.
4. **Shape the cookies**: Roll the dough into 1-inch balls and roll them in the remaining 1/2 cup of sugar. Place them on a baking sheet about 2 inches apart.
5. **Bake**: Bake for 8-10 minutes, or until the edges are lightly golden. Let cool on the baking sheet for a few minutes before transferring to a wire rack to cool completely.
6. **Serve**: Enjoy as a sweet treat for the holidays!